Animals on the Move

By Allan Fowler

Consultants

Linda Cornwell, Coordinator of School Quality
and Professional Improvement
Indiana State Teachers Association

Jan Jenner, Ph.D.

Children's Press®
A Division of Grolier Publishing
New York   London   Hong Kong   Sydney
Danbury, Connecticut

Visit Children's Press® on the Internet at:
http://publishing.grolier.com

Designer: Herman Adler Design Group
Photo Researcher: Caroline Anderson
The photo on the cover of this book shows a flock of migrating snow geese.

Library of Congress Cataloging-in-Publication Data

Fowler, Allan.
    Animals on the move / by Allan Fowler.
      p. cm. — (Rookie read-about science)
    Includes index.
    Summary: Discusses how and why various animals migrate,
moving in a group from place to place seeking food and better weather.
    ISBN 0-516-21589-2 (lib. bdg.)   0-516-27056-9 (pbk.)
    1. Animal migration—Juvenile literature. [1. Animals—Migration.]
I. Titles. II. Series.
QL754.F68   2000   98-52944
591.56'8—dc21   CIP
                                       AC

GROLIER
PUBLISHING

All animals, including people, are on the move. Birds fly, cheetahs run, and fish swim.

In Africa, wildebeest migrate to find food.

In spring and autumn,
some animals make
long trips.

They migrate from place
to place to look for food,
lay eggs, or give birth.

Arctic terns migrate alone. They fly farther than any other bird.

Arctic tern

The albatross uses its long wings to fly over the ocean.

9

Snow geese

Many birds travel in big groups called flocks.

Ducks and geese fly south every autumn to find food.

They fly north every spring to lay eggs.

How do birds know
which way to fly?

Scientists aren't sure.
Some may follow the
sun and stars.

Others may use rivers
or mountains as a guide.

Geese form a V-shape when they migrate.

Burchell's zebras

Birds are not the only
animals that migrate.

Zebras travel across
Africa in large herds.

In North America,
moose, elk, and
caribou may migrate.

A herd of caribou

Mountain goat

Mountain goats migrate to escape cold weather. They move down to lower ground.

Every autumn, monarch butterflies travel south.

They spend the winter in Florida, southern California, or Mexico.

Monarch butterflies

Atlantic salmon

Salmon swim out to sea
when they are young.

Later, they migrate to the
river where they grew
up and lay eggs.

To swim upstream, the salmon may have to leap over strong waves.

Salmon swimming upstream

A female humpback whale with her calf

In the spring, whales
swim north and eat
tiny ocean creatures.

In autumn, they migrate
south to warmer waters
and give birth.

Animals have been migrating for thousands of years.

Someday scientists may learn how animals know when to leave, where to go, and how to get there.

African elephants migrate to find food.

Words You Know

albatross

Arctic tern

Atlantic salmon

caribou

snow geese

wildebeest

Index

About the Author

Allan Fowler is a freelance writer with a background in advertising.
Born in New York, he now lives in Chicago and enjoys traveling.

Photo Credits

©: Dembinsky Photo Assoc.: 18 (Alan G. Nelson); ENP Images: 9, 14, 29,
30 top left (Gerry Ellis); Marine Mammal Images: 26 (Michael Nolan); Peter
Arnold Inc.: 21 (James L. Amos), 17, 30 bottom left (Joel Bennett), 4, 31 bottom
(BIOS/M&C Denis Huot), 22, 31 top right (Schafer & Hill), 10, 30 bottom right
(Gunter Ziesler); Photo Researchers: 7, 30 top right (Stephen Dalton), 3 (Tim
Davis), cover (Pat & Tom Leeson), 25 (Ronald Thompson); Tony Stone Images:
13, 31 top left (Tim Davis).